Of Pen and Ink
and Paper Scraps

by LUCIEN STRYK

SWALLOW PRESS

OHIO UNIVERSITY PRESS

ATHENS

Swallow Press/Ohio University Press books
are printed on acid-free paper ∞

Library of Congress Cataloging-in-Publication Data
Stryk, Lucien.
    Of pen and ink and paper scraps / by Lucien Stryk.
        p.   cm.
    ISBN 0-8040-0918-X (alk paper). —ISBN 0-8040 -0919-8 (pbk. :
alk. paper)
    I. Title.
PS3569.T7604   1989
811'.54   89-4110
                                                              CIP

Designed by Laury A. Egan

FOR HELEN

FELLOW IN ALL I DO

Contents

Acknowledgments

For permission to use poems which first appeared in
their pages thanks are due to the editors of *American
Poetry Review, The Bloomsbury Review, Encounter,
Calliope, Chariton Review, The Cream City Review,
London Magazine, Mid-American Review, Midnight
Lamp, Outlet, Poetry* ("Botanist," copyright 1987,
"Dreaming to Music," copyright 1988, and "Light,"
copyright 1989, Modern Poetry Association), *Raccoon,*
and *Whetstone.* I am most grateful to Noboru Fujiwara
for help with the Issa poems.

Of Pen and Ink and Paper Scraps

Yet why not say what happened?
Pray for the grace of accuracy
Vermeer gave to the sun's illumination
stealing like the tide across a map . . .

— ROBERT LOWELL, "Epilogue"

ONE

From the Window

Luck—1932

After the market crash, everyone
short on luck, I squinted out
my bedroom window for the last time,

holding the rabbit's foot I'd
swopped my slingshot for, counted
numbers for a miracle that wouldn't

come. As the last mock-orange
petal in Andrade's yard spun into
summer, the junkman divvied up

our table, chairs, beds, all we
could not cart off from Chicago, for
a piddling sum. Clutching my can

of marbles, baseball mitt, I followed
mother lugging my baby sister,
worldly goods stuffed in a canvas

bag. Tracking my father, job to
job, St. Louis to Columbus. All
that year I made spells, counting

heads, trees, fireflies, polished my
wishbone seven times, again. Until
I landed back in the old city,

raced to Washington Park, joined my
playmates, Shorty, Tonsils, Mike,
riding Taft's human pyramid of *Time.*

As I explained how luck had brought
us back, I found real magic, twigs
sparkling into flower before my eyes.

Black Monday

(NYC, October 1987)

After an early morning trek
under a spill of trees
anchored in rock, where sky-
beams blue as chicory outline

palisades along the Hudson's
bank across the way, I take
the A-train down to 42nd Street.
Across the aisle a young man

beats a rhythm with his feet,
mouthing the rap. As we speed
on, faster, even faster goes
his song. Indifferent to eyes

blinking over headlines of the
market crash, faces grim
as bogs, his soul's raw poem
belts out its need from stop

to stop. Doors open, slam and
open. He takes off, jiving
down the platform toward
gray streets of unending sound.

Light

There comes a moment, turning
a corner sharply, I run
into a young delivery boy on

his first summer job, carting
kegs of white lead, cans of paint
in a red wagon, once his toy,

to patrons of his father's store.
Passing the quips and clowning
of his one-time friends, munching

his wage of cookies, apples, candy,
pocketing a nickle at some doorway
now and then. There comes a time

I see my own face in that twelve
year old, steering his cargo by
the blind man with a caged canary

pecking fortunes typed on colored
paper for a dime. Tempted to stop
he scoots along, afraid to know

how places will dissolve in time,
turn up fifty years later in
a certain light, here on my desk.

My Father Reading

Whenever I catch my father
nodding over endless books—

Grass, Montherlant, Moravia,
Camus—I wonder what he read

the day my mother, who had seen
the stern-eyed soldier at

his desk while on some long-
forgotten errand for a brother,

turned up at the army camp to
entertain the conscripts with

her joyous recitation of folk
poems. Was it that night her

image leapt from some page of
philosophy or art—

led to the moment I could voice
their lives in this brief song.

From the Window

After night's news stories:
senseless slaughter,
politicking, hunger, waste,

with hype and sport thrown
in, once more to wake
as sun kindles the linden,

lilac, willow-oak, catches
the red-cap drilling layered
membrane of the old pear bark.

So many season's rounds of
twig, bud, flower, fruit
have made a banquet for this

stiff-tailed guzzler, now
well slaked, strut-drumming
on a branch to lure his mate.

Dreaming to Music

Windstorm thrums
the window, drizzles
the maple's flame.

So begins another
summer's end. As I
turn up the stereo

a girl in Rheims
walks out of a medieval
love song, lifts

her brocaded gown
along the mucky path
out of the woods,

shortcutting through
a wheatfield silvered
in cloudburst, toward

the farmhouse gate.
Flicking the latch she
looks back, whispers

her passion to the rain,
this Sunday afternoon,
six centuries late.

Scrap Paper

I'm strapped into the oral
surgeon's bogey-chair. The scene
of Northern woods upon the wall

swirls into years of pipe smoke
as the needle hits the dark
vein of my hand, sends me groping

over mounds of textbook
galley sheets, generously donated
by a friend. The brambled

type threads business jargon
through my images, whips pines,
percentiles, graphs into one puff.

So much for more than thirty years
of fine-cut Latakia, sweet
Virginia. As finger-printed carbons

fill my lesioned roof of mouth,
I choke off dark, somehow to
find a clearing where I stumble on

the arms of wife and son, back to
a woozy world of masks made up
of pen and ink and paper scraps.

New Roof

Tarred roof's done: now squirrels,
birds can stop off as they please.

Rap of crabapple, twig, descant of
sleet and gale won't frazzle us again.

Sipping tea, I contemplate old rain-
spots on the ceiling, tune smugly

into newscasts brewing storms. My
peace is startled by wild sounds

behind the furnace-closet door. Wonder
what poor ghost would bother with

a house lacking a basement or dark
winding stairs. Open up, warily look

around, follow a trail of feathers to
a songless wren cowed in the chimney

corner. I open windows, doors, pull
off the screens. Coax, plead and point

the way. Offer my palm. I stalk it,
scoop it tenderly, set it outside before

the maple. Watch it soar, then flounder
back to earth, where from the bushes

a marauding tabby pounces. Later,
I find a tawny feather in the grass.

Misty Morning

The bluejay leaps in/out
vague rakings of the long ago.

Brief photos skelter by,
so many squirrel generations

back in time. Our children
once again are those small

armfuls we might dream would
stay. Our son, racing me

up the mountain path (I let
him sprint ahead), to reach

the Shinto Shrine. Joyfully
there he tries to capture

bubbles of reflected light
between his hands. The memory

turns. I'm sledding with our
girl, warmed by her spirit.

Down she tumbles, laughing,
auburn hair like flame against

the snow. Deep in this sacred
album mists rise, fall about

the trees that are, that were—
cover the distance of our

paths, now that the years
have made us what we are.

Star

Easing out of the garage
toward the emptied garbage
cans field-basing barbered
lawns, ceramic doodads, shrubs,
petunias and geranium beds

half circling downhill, I pull
up sharply as the red-haired
girl across the street turns
up the volume of her boom-box
to full blast, limps out into

the pathway, flexing the braces
on her gammy knees, spits
in her mitt, eager to be
first woman in the baseball
Hall of Fame. Touched by

her gesture, as if she's asking
why the world won't stop to
play, I pull up to the curb,
shut off the motor and, despite
the fussbudget behind the louvered

blinds next door, I nab a fast
one, watch the bittersweet
surprise turn to anticipation,
taking on her pop-idol's
applause as she dreams, base

to base, her first homerun.

Wind Chime

Wind stirs a bonfire of
October maples. I take off
with my daughter, son, his

wife and son, for woods on
Indian river. Years we've
trespassed through this maze

of creatures, sharing wild
grapes, walnuts, mushroom
puffs. Tangling with hail-fellow

mosquitoes. Tracked through
snowdrifts, storms, up to this
stand of poplars, listening

to wind-chime icicles. Today
as autumn shreds and patches up,
we hear the strumming leaves,

watch branches weaving light
into the clouds, know each time
we return might be the last.

Walkers

In sun, in snow, after dawn's
daily dozen on the page,
I shove off down the hill,

take in the same three walkers
circling the park, alongside
gopher lookouts in the scrub.

Safe from the news, day's
tally of brutality and greed,
I catch an acorn's fall, step

over a leaf, nod at the old
man with the fat, lame dog
in tow, smile at the woman

in the sweatsuit with the sad
drawn face, wave as the middle-
ager, bobbing to his headphones,

passes by. Along the quiet
path thoughts fracture, fly
to where a flock of crows mob

a lone owl reflecting in the oak.

Garage Sale

. . . so the nightmare enters
where I wait the rummagers

hunched in a beat-up lawnchair,
feet astride the oil-smudge

on the floor. A car pulls up,
a critic's eyes lynx through

the windshield and the motor
churns, roars off. Well,

I'm just a jingler sharing
the dust with spiders, come

with over sixty years of
misplaced images, not everybody's

bargain. A whitehaired couple
drop in, regard me with suspicion—

what a pity I am not their long
lost son. Take me, I say. Come

buy nothing for nothing, poems
thrown in free. As they fade out

I take the garage sale sign
down, hope for a better day.

Latest News

The Hubbard Glacier, 80 miles
long, 360 feet tall,
is splitting from Alaska,

threatening ocean levels,
sending tremors through
the markets of the world.

Seas will flush out factories,
centuries of masterworks,
blueprints for doom into

the sludge. Igloo and mansion,
barrack and doss-house will
make a new Atlantis, moldy

with warheads, yo-yos, monuments
stockpiling barnacles,
leaving no trace. Sanctuaries

are tipped off to go under,
sending waves of walrus, polar
bear and sprat over seawalls.

Meanwhile as the glacier surges
14 yards a day, ticker-tapes
snake onto desks of speculators,

land values of mountains swell
their dreams. From the Rockies,
Alps, the Urals up to Katmandu,

who knows—if cities, forests,
valleys disappear—Mount Ararat
might come into its own again?

May Day

With spring flowers,
year by year, I watch
the pretty youngster from

the house behind our yard
tiptoeing past the window,
leaving a May-basket at

our door. This time a
paper cone with golden
streamers, colored candies,

chocolate kisses, gum
and purple lilac, to delight
us for the day. Such quiet,

such innocence. Yet each
year brings her closer
to the instant when despair

butts in on joy, opens
the window on harsh May
Days, where empty baskets

hold the hunger of a world.

Theo

Old folk squinting on a bench
    outside the Lodge,
hands folded, feet in line,

shrink into afternoon, like
    Michelangelo's
snowmen carved for a famous

garden on a vain Medici's whim.
    They perk up
as my grandson greets them,

whizzing by on his red bike—
    fleeting reminder
of a small boy round the corner

of their years. Soon he'll grow
    off from us,
this eight year old, his violin

bow already drifting from a squeaky
    exercise into
Bach minuets. I'll miss our

secret tales—audacious clowns,
    mischievous bears.
Quick-freeze his laughter, goodnight

kisses for the day I lean,
    ice-sculptured
on some bench, waiting the thaw.

Daffodils, Irises

My wife's gift—

a birthday halo,
yellow/purple,
trembling from
the Yamaguchi vase
upon my desk.

Saying, year by
year find words
to equal these,
beyond the fallen
petal, withered stalk.

Thoughts Before Travel

Baggage stacked and labeled,
phone, cable-television cut off,
disconnecting our small lodging

from the world, I wait the ride
into the airport in the backyard
by the trees. Snip-snipping

of a neighbor's shears, first
spring cough of a mower grow
remote, as bluebird, redbird

sky-dance over iris, and a rabbit
bolts under the grapevine tangle
by the garden shed. Moments of

past journeys stir with laughter
of our children as we pitch on narrow
benches in a third-class carriage

from Bombay up to the Elephanta Caves.
Or enter gardens of raked sand
and stone, stroll under pines to

picnic in the shade of the great
Kamakura Buddha. Follow a desert,
tracing Assassin castles into Zahidan.

Rambling on, a car horn blasts me
back into our rhubarb jungle where
frogs, gorging insects, croak farewell.

June 5, 1987

While I wash dishes to
Gregorian chants, what
started out a ho-hum
day—the usual round

of doodles, chores,
anxieties—explodes
with a bright swallowtail
joyriding by the window,

looping where by whitest
columbines a robin, head
cocked to love sounds,
watches as a squirrel

near the old pear tree
quivers astride his mate.
The phone rings, bringing
word Shinkichi Takahashi

died last night.
                And so
the world goes on. Now
the squirrels scamper

through the branches,
making leaves dance
like the poet's sparrows
wing-stroking an elegy in air.

Translating Zen Poems

(I. M. Takashi Ikemoto)

The sliding doors open in
the house hugging the mountain-
side where my children sled

in sandpapered orange-crates,
downswoop into our garden under
snow-glazed cypress, walnut,

fig, persimmon trees, mowing
dried stalks of tall eulalia
grass along the way. Inside,

we sit crosslegged, flushed
with hibachi embers, before
the plum-black Sado vase,

under your gift, the Taiga
scroll plum-blossoming out of
season. Over green tea and sweet

bean cake, I watch you shuffling
pages where I've englished
sparrows, temple gardens, fish,

time, universe—waiting
your word.
              Now, thumbing through

years of those poems, I see you,
old friend, in flickering
light of sunset over snow-roofs

of this midwest town, recall
a moment under a mountain, when we
knew a master's words need never die.

TWO

Issa: A Suite
of Haiku

Passing wild geese,
lighting night
mountains of Shinano.

Even in warmest
glow, how
cold my shadow.

Welcome,
wild geese—
now you are Japan's.

In spring rain
how they carry on,
uneaten ducks.

Over fading
eulalia,
cold's white ghost.

Snowy fields—
now rice is down,
more geese than men.

Vines tight
around scorched rocks—
midday glories.

Moist spring moon—
raise a finger
and it drips.

Cooling melon—
at a hint of footsteps,
you're a frog.

My village
traced through haze—
still an eyesore.

Good world—
grass field swollen
with dumplings.

Silverfish escaping—
mothers,
fathers, children.

Sprawled like an X—
how carefree,
how lonely.

Melting snow—
the village flows
with children.

Winter's here—
around the fire,
stench of gossip.

Telescope—
eyeful of haze,
three pence.

Dawn—fog
of Mt. Asama spreads
on my table.

"Gray starling!"
they sneer behind me,
freezing the bone.

House burnt down—
fleas
dance in embers.

My old home—
wherever I touch,
thorns.

Rustling
the grassy field—
departing spring.

Fuji dusk—
back to back,
frogs are chanting.

Far over the
withered field,
light from a hut.

My limbs sharp
as iron nails,
in autumn wind.

Watch out,
young sparrows—
Prince Horse trots close.

Each time I swat
a fly, I squint
at the mountain.

Back gate opens
itself—
how long the day.

Evening—above
kitchen smoke and my
poor knees, wild geese!

Playing stone,
frog lets
the horse sniff.

Don't kill the fly—
it wrings
its hands, its feet.

High on the hill,
I cough
into the autumn gust.

Great moon
woven in plum scent,
all mine.

Song of skylark—
night falls
from my face.

After night in
the dog's bowl,
butterfly scoots off.

Cherry blossoms
everywhere: this
undeserving world.

Frog and I,
eyeball
to eyeball.

Winter moon—
outer moat
cracks with cold.

Woodpecker on
the temple pillar—
die! die! die!

What a moon—
if only she were here,
my bitter wife.

My thinning hair,
eulalia grass,
rustling together.

Plum in bloom—
the Gates of Hell
stay shut.

Charcoal fire—
spark by spark,
we fade too.

Morning glory—
whose face
is without fault?

Wonderful—
under cherry blossoms,
this gift of life.

New Year's Day—
blizzard of
plum blossoms.

Snail—baring
shoulders
to the moon.

My empty face,
betrayed
by lightning.

Into the house
before me,
fly on my hat.

Snail—
always
at home.

Temple gong frozen—
this side of the mountain
I shiver in bed.

Snail, finding
the path
to my foot.

Where in the galaxy
docs it wait,
my wandering star?

Autumn wind—
once, it too
was fresh.

Splash—
crow into
white dew.

Sadness of cool
melons—two days
nobody's come.

Autumn mountain—
"We're still alive up here,"
boom temple gongs.

Evening cherry blooms—
is today
really yesterday?

Strong wind—
dog drags
two samurai.

Moonlit wall—
frozen shadow
of the pine.

Bright moon,
welcome to my hut—
such as it is.

Milky Way—windbags
in the capital
struck dumb by you.

Shower: caught in
lightning flash—
me, the death-hater.

Poor winter village—
frosted on notice-board:
"No charity."

Summer field—
thunder,
or my empty stomach?

Cool breeze,
tangled
in a grass-blade.

Short night: snoring
under trees, on rocks—
traveling priests.

Plum blossom branch—
moon urges me
to steal you.

Plum scent—
guests won't mind
the chipped cup.

Praying mantis—
one hand
on temple bell.

Haze swirling
the gate—
who comes?

Light haze—
his sedge hat
waving goodbye.

World of dew?
Perhaps,
and yet. . . .

THREE

The Blue Tower

Three Saints of
Nardo di Cione

(painted in Florence, 1350)

What an eye for color! I remember
those three saints in softest
green, rose, blue flushed robes

staring raptly at me—as if
we were close-knit, elbows touching,
silent together 650 years. Have

they mused on this selfsame face
over the ages, through tyrannies,
uprisings, famines, searching in

the wrong place for the Fountain
of Forever? Unlike these park-
squatter pigeons, whirring content

past the lily-pond by late-summer
goatsbeard, from bench to bench,
cocksure of offerings. Soon they

will take off, soar beyond nests
in thick trees to the shoulders
of saints, feathers soft green,

rose and blue, in unfading light.

Salvator Rosa (1615–73)

Strong sun on the Tuscan
town where he painted
did not flush the somber

face of his revolutionist
(that head meant for axing)
propped on the easel, rough

hands unrolling a banner
with—goosequilled in
haste—"Silence, unless

what you have to say
is better than silence."
As sunlight entangled the

hills inquisitors ranted,
rebellion was whispered in
shade. Rosa worked on, deepening

eyes of his saints, risking
slogans on canvas. And
that was better than silence.

Modern Art

The lumpish woman
with such grief carved
in her face, cardigan

stretched out of shape
draping her rounded
shoulders over a bargain-

basement dress, stands
in a corner of the
gallery, indifferent

to know-alls solving
nothing before Pollocks,
Klines, De Koonings,

stopping by to touch
her, snigger at her need
to find the Way Out

of this bitter world,
crumble back to
powder, start again.

Fame

Snow on chalet roofs dazzles
as the Paris-Rome Express
scorches the passes. Crammed

with a Turkish widow and her
pouting son in a couchette,
I sip her offering, a paper

cup of wine, answer questions
vaguely, staring out at Swiss Alps
candling the sky. "To Florence,

and alone, for Dante? Ha!"
Suddenly she points a finger
at me, says, "My friend, there

is a Turkish poet greater . . .
taller than these mountains
over pygmy rocks." Stirred

by her passion the boy forgets
to whine, fidgets with glee.
She hands me pen and paper—

"Your address," she says, "I'll
send . . . you'll see!" I
drain the cup, decline another

drop. Lean back and close my
eyes until we reach the border.
Watch her take off, boy in tow.

She turns back, waves, and calls—
"You'll see. There's no one like
him. Never . . . never will be."

Venice

Boozy on art, I savor
my *espresso* at an outdoor
cafe in St. Mark's Square.

Observe the camera touts
snapping peanut vendors
as they hustle tourists among

pigeons, under the unflinching
eye of a winged lion
and St. Theodore astride

his crocodile. As six
musicians strike a barcarole
I squint at light on

stone, the roundabout
of faces as sun slips
down cathedral columns.

Dozing off, I am Francesco
Guardi painting out
the four bronze horses

from the tiered roof of
St. Mark's, down to the
square, where I must return

them over the canals
to Constantinople—
there my canvas waits.

The Savior of Hyde Park

Years, at Speaker's Corner,
he offered reason to
the crowds, at a respectful

distance on a crate he'd
bought for sixpence from
a tout. Shuffling ideas

on weather, politics, art,
war, old Shakespeare
and the like, he held sway

over "Hear hears," "Quite
Sos," hecklers. An encore for
a handshake was his rule.

Squinting at notes to check
a point, thumbs in lapels,
he'd pause for laughs or cheers.

Until the mood changed with
the times—sneers, insults,
lewd remarks forced his escape.

Nowadays he stands alone upon
his perch, tattered notes rolled
tightly in one hand, the other

at his chest. Silent, he
stares out at an audience of
trees, a sculpture of a man

returned to save the world.

Legacy

I look outside where the once
scurvy crook-shaped plot,
cooped by a stark brick wall—

breathing space of semi-basement
flats—has turned into
an Eden. Think of the grayhaired

woman up in Number 8, who
three years earlier shrugged at
apartment-ruled "off limits,"

neighbors' slights behind
drawn curtains. Set to
with spade and trowel, digging,

planting, watering seedlings,
pointing out sproutings to her
old lamed husband, stooping to

weed, pick up a cigarette butt
contemptuously aimed. Widowed
since, gone to a "sheltered lodge,"

I wonder if she's thinking this
midsummer of a wall ablaze with
roses, lupines, daisies, pinks,

hydrangeas shimmering like
stained glass against worn brick?
Now from behind those windows,

drapes flung wide, the undeserving
gape, where fragrant and bee-
swarmed, buds open to the sun.

Friends

Arm in arm the two men
enter Regent's Park,
cross the bridge of flared

geraniums, horned lupines
and the trail of lavender
to the stone-shelved

waterfall, pausing to
chat under a thatch of
willow. Then on to lush

Bird Island, gesturing
where duck families
pass fiery-beaked black

swans close by the reeds.
The blind man glances
through his friend's eyes

at the sweetpea trellis,
flush of roses, madcap
columbines. Settling on

a bench they shower crumbs
to birds, rejoice together
as a sparrow chances on the

blind one's outstretched hand.

Hove Beach

(after John Constable)

The woman in the wide-
brimmed hat down on

the beach, squints over
the surf, no longer in

hope of reunion. Her
boy, in starched sailor

suit, still believes
the world he maps out

in the sand will survive
the walloping tides.

As sunset dissolves
in waves, the painter

dips his brush in
the wash of horizon,

sends fishing boats
over the canvas edge.

Bacchus

Coaxing a skirl from
his harmonica, the tippler

in the grime-stiff coat
riling commuters by

the station gate, two-steps
backwards off the curb,

rights himself, shakes
windmill fists at life,

the world, the mob who
will not pause to throw

a pittance, to tot up
his night. Blowed if he

cares just how they waste
their lives, shoving in

and out of doors rigged up
to slam shut in one's

face. It serves them
right, snubbing a thirsty man.

Landscape

Over the twilight field
the lost, the fortunate
have wandered paths,
slowly exited the gates,

yet flute-notes hover in
the outlined plane trees,
latticed reflections
of the sky, crisscrossed

by gulls that drift close
to the young man sprawled
on a park bench, flute
bronzed in sun's last rays.

From zoo cages, just over
the fence, roarers,
bleaters, trumpeters answer,
each with his simple need.

Surprise

While his mother sunbathes
full-length on the grass
beside the lily-pond in

St. John's Garden, the small
boy begs rose cuttings of
the gardener snipping among

August beds. His hands flutter
over the basket like twin
butterflies as he picks out

red, orange, yellow petals,
sniffing each windfall in
delight. Hands full, he frisks

back to his mother, places
them gently on her legs, arms,
makes a garland for her hair.

Night Music

The artist rousing a Chopin
polonaise on stage, at Royal
Festival Hall, is tuned out
of the drama stirring under

the concrete columns below,
the hum of the anywhere-sleepers
bearing their worldly
bundles, their cardboard cots.

Settling in chosen corners
out of the wind, these minstrels
of hazy wine-moons nod off
as a fiddler close by the bridge

waits on the concert crowd's
exit, the generous few, tunes up
his strings, sets his cap down
and fingers a waltz to the river.

Drama

The white hairpiece he
wears for his part
in the play down the road

is no disguise for the
veteran actor slipping
unnoticed into a rear seat

at a rival's matinee.
Collar up, he improvises
a fresh plot where, as

lights dim, a swarm of
eager faces turn back from
the stage to cheer him

through his consummate role—
funny, relentless, spell-
binding, drawing their

laughter, sighs, bravos with
a mere gesture. As the curtain
rises and the scene takes

shape, he knows the audience
he loved for loving him
have found a new face to betray.

Images

I

Glimpsed through
rushes fringing

the duckpond isle,
a Japanese

lantern feathered
with goosedown,

image capsized
in water-light.

Ruffling before it
a young gray-lag

gander beats
territorial waves.

II

The train jolts me
to an awareness

of gulls, hundreds
of them, fresh from

oil-rig furrows of
the North Sea. They

dive to barley fields,
close to the plow

churning black waves
from earth—

then veer to clouds
with their spoil.

Botanist

(Sweden, 1986)

The season leaning into
winter in Uppsala, my friend
    Lennart and I

warm up with coffee in
a second-floor cafe. Look
    out the window

at the year-end remnants
of Linnaeus' Garden, speak
    of the harmony

of rows, the rage for order.
Remembering the Latin cry
    for Clarity, I

see now what I lack, wonder
why this handsome young
    translator of plays

and poems chose to take on
a voice lost in wild and
    unnamed grasses where

birds, so namelessly alive,
return from unknown regions every
    spring, to swoop

where gold untitled flowers
light leaf-fossils through
    old winter's mud.

Fishing with Casper

(Sweden, 1986)

Ringed by shadow-heads of pines
we drift over Stromaren, Lake of Storms,
in bright nippy air, trailing

Old Pike, the one who never fails
to get away. Casper gives
the rod to me, hoping for stranger's

luck, rows us from point to point
where, he says, fish abound. As
the line grows heavy I pull in my catch,

a clump of tangled reeds. Through
the swift-darkening afternoon, forest
closing in, my friend consoles me,

certain there will be no fish-fry
back in Orbyhus tonight, where his wife
and children wait us in their sprawling

house inside the castle grounds. There,
over schnapps, sharp herring, moose,
crisp tart snowberries we laugh together,

chat of icefishing and poems, canny pike
and bass, still warmed by light-arrows
piercing water, a moment of October sun.

The Blue Tower

(Sweden, 1986)

Uninvited, up in the Blue Tower
we touch four years of a man's
life. Strindberg's last home,
on Drottninggatan: those

stage-prop rooms, rigidly ordered
desk, photos of wives, a laurel
wreath framing his youngest child,
cheap casts of artists that he

must have loved one time, third-
rate wallhangings—caves, fluted
columns, backdrops for scenes—,
shadows of masterworks. And all

the rivalries, a melancholia
that poisoned fame, seeping through
doors, following into afternoon
streets of Old Stockholm. On

to evening at the Royal Theater
where I feel Miss Julie's passion,
in a language I can't follow, more
intense than ever. Watch the spit-

booting servant edge from cunning
into scorn, catch the rancor in him,
the despair in her. Outside, walking
with friends back to my lodging,

we pass where Olof Palme, strolling
out of a theater with his wife, met
his assassin. On that very spot
his mourners place fresh roses every day.

Before a Reading

(On the Day of the Mini-Summit,
October 11, 1986)

To turn away, not to be overcome
here in Sweden, quietest of lands,

as earth opens in San Salvador
swallowing rightists, leftists,

whipping the rage of 60,000 perished
in civil war into one scream—

will they turn away? Or pause
to remember the quake last year

in Mexico City, leaving an old man
blinking through space, once home,

weeping for songs left unsung by
children, grandchildren? Will they

black out the volcano spilt over
orchards bursting with sweetness

for 400 years in Colombia, where all
that remained was the petrified

arm of a woman reaching from lava
in hope? Is it to warn, this ice-rain

mantling shoulders of those gone
to barter the world in Reykjavik

while wolves prowl pine mountains
of Nerrbotten, howl at an empty sky?